HOUSE

200 ideas to declutter your home, room by room

Contents

Text by Sara Burford.

This edition published in 2008 by L&K Designs.

PRINTED IN CHINA

Publishers Disclaimer

The uses, hints, tips and ideas contained in this book are passed on in good faith but the publisher cannot be held responsible for any adverse results.

Domestic bliss or room for improvement?

When you imagine the arrival of unexpected guests what gut reaction does that conjure up in you? Are you filled with the warm, fuzzy feelings of expectation at the imminent arrival of close friends or loved ones? Are you happy and content with the layout and interior of your home, enough so that you've time for a change of clothes, a new layer of lippy and a nonchalant plumping of pillows?...

Or, like most of us, are you filled with complete horror and despair at the disarray and chaos which is known as 'your-house', currently bearing a far too uncomfortable resemblance to a war-zone? And will you be fast considering turning out the lights, lying on your living room floor, (and ordering everyone else in the house to do so; including the unsuspecting gasman), and pretending that no-one is in?

Safe to say that the latter of these two scenarios is certainly more widely experienced and feelings of angst-ridden guilt at not having a tidy-clean house is fast becoming the status quo of our ever-busy, overly-cluttered and frantically-paced modern lives.

As inhabitants of the 21st century we are considered to 'have-it-all' – but have we really? Do we have the basic conserves of time and energy to live our lives in the way we once envisaged? Or are we constantly battling with an ever growing workload of balancing busy jobs, carrying out domestic chores and duties; and most importantly, taking physical and emotional care of our families? It can feel a lot like shovelling snow in the midst of a never-ending blizzard – no wonder our homes get cluttered from being in constant competition with all these other demands.

Entertaining at home used to be an enjoyable and popular pastime, one which has fast diminished over the last few decades. The reason? Simply, time and energy. It's a researched fact that we now have more than ever to do and less time to do it all in. Many of us have neither the time nor the energy, not only in making the effort to socialise, but in undertaking the sheer amount of hard work that goes into tidying and cleaning our houses to an 'acceptable' standard for our guests – which can realistically be an all day event.

In an age obsessed with aesthetics we have become paralysed by our fear of what others might think and equally overwhelmed by our insistence to 'do' as much as possible, without taking time out to just be ourselves and enjoy life. There seems a dire need to get back to basics and do what we can to uncomplicate, de-stress and streamline our lives. Detoxing your house seems like as good a place as any to start!

When you look at your home today do you feel happy and relaxed, in control and surrounded by possessions that you love and enjoy; possessions that reflect who you and your family are in your lives today? If not, then clutter may well be a central issue for you.

Do you hang onto and hoard stuff you really don't need? Maybe it's a long-term habit formed for a now long forgotten reason, or maybe you understand why you do it, but don't feel you know any other way of being – or maybe it's just plain scary to think of changing things so radically.

Whatever the reason, the fact is that constantly expending energy on things that clutter and create disorder in our surroundings; and inevitably our minds, is nothing short of exhausting. Living with and having to avoid clutter slows us down, however we choose to look at it.

Our homes are where we get to be ourselves and relax. Ideally our homes should feel welcoming, comfortable and happy. This way we will want to spend time together as families and friends, in a positive and pleasant atmosphere. Unfortunately, when our homes are cluttered and disordered this generally extends to, and affects household members adversely, discouraging quality time together and creating a stressful environment.

Clutter lends itself to old habits, lifestyles, ideas and possessions. This in turn suffocates creativity, inspiration and new ways of thinking and being. No wonder we get stuck in a rut when we're surrounded by too much 'stuff'. However, in defense of getting to this point, to some extent it's completely normal to accumulate possessions that we don't need. Clutter has an innate way of building quietly and steadily without our really paying attention. What once had a purpose, practical use or creative direction gradually loses meaning, and it can be all too easy not to notice.
But eventually this lack of awareness can spiral out of control and before we know it we're living in virtual chaos without any clear idea of how we got there or how to resolve it.

This book is for anyone who wants to take the first tentative steps in tackling what seems to be the impossible, by creating a more spacious and organised environment for themselves and their families.

Starting at the beginning, we'll look at what clutter is and how much is realistic to expect in our lives, after-all it's unreasonable for us to aim for pristine perfection 24/7, (that would be more than just a little eerie!). We'll go on to look at how we can unwittingly find ourselves in the midst of a clutter-nightmare and the negative affect that can have on our lives, and ultimately moving onto the many benefits of undertaking a decluttering campaign, followed by room-by-room steps and useful tips in achieving a more streamlined way of house-keeping.

Decluttering is an ongoing way of life, a renewed state of mind which will thrive on creating new ideas and activities. So it's time to unload all that unnecessary emotional baggage of stress, confusion and frustration and work towards a more effective, fulfilled and happy household.

Make a start

Make a start

What is clutter?

Clutter can be characterised by a multitude of 'sins' – messy rooms, jumbled drawers, disorganised wardrobes, random stacks of books, magazines and papers, piles of letters, documents and junk mail, plastic food containers that just might come in handy, a plethora of expired kitchen, bathroom and beauty products, clothes you can't bear to part with, surfaces that haven't been seen for a number of years under goodness-knows-what, floors covered in discarded clothes, stuff' underneath beds – which, if in a house inhabited by teens, will possibly have some previously undiscovered form of fungi or revolutionary new antibiotic moulded permanently to what once resembled a plate – you get the general picture?

In essence, clutter pretty much covers anything that: -

- doesn't have a current or foreseen use or has gone past its 'use by' date
- you don't like the look of, (including unwanted gifts)
- blocks, covers or spills over into areas of the house which would otherwise be utilised for other uses
- is broken and either can't or isn't going to be mended
- prevents you from living in an easily accessible, organised and structured way

Clutter is certainly nothing if not easy to accumulate, but not quite so easy to clear once it's taken a hold. It's often a quick and easy solution to move clutter to an available, momentarily convenient place, with the best intentions to move it at a later point. Or to glance at your 10th magazine subscription and convince yourself that you'll read it later, when you've had time to read the others... Of course, we all know how such good intentions can lose their way. Suffice to say clutter is more of a widespread issue than many of us think, with most of us having to deal with it at some point in our lives to lesser or greater degrees.

Clutter is tangible evidence of many things: poor or misguided domestic habits, chronic lack of organisaton, the inability to say 'No', too many sentimental attachments, hoarding habits and even just sheer laziness. But at the heart of all clutter is procrastination and many, many decisions that have yet to be made.

Resistance is futile!

For some, actually taking ownership of the fact that there is a clutter problem can be terribly disconcerting and stir up feelings of uncomfortable embarrassment, which may then manifest in feelings of denial. Once we are in denial we face yet another challenge, in that it's impossible to change what we don't acknowledge – simply, if you refuse to believe there's an issue then nothing will get done! So taking personal responsibility and being honest with ourselves is vital to any clearing-out process. If you're not sure where you stand, then talk to someone close to you, someone whose opinion and judgment you trust and respect. But be prepared to hear the truth!

Feeling resistance to such a fundamental change in how you live your life is completely natural, as are feelings of anxiety. Although we may essentially want to make major changes, human nature determines that we are somehow more comfortable with what's familiar to us – even if that familiarity means chaos! The unknown and potential for living life differently can be daunting, so accept any resistance you may feel as normal; you're courageous and you WILL be okay.

What's a realistic amount of clutter?

As much as we might fantasise about an eternally tidy and organised house, we know that it is in fact a physical impossibility and a 'reality' confined only to glossy magazines and showrooms. Having such high expectations can be a source of stress in itself and a further drain of energy – not to mention the tension it may cause other members of the household if they are constantly being nagged over the smallest perceived domestic-offences. And realistically, would we really want our lives to be that pristine and clinical?

A welcoming house looks warm, inviting and lived in, with visible and tangible signs of life. How do we feel if we walk into a house where the sofa looks like it's never been sat on, the carpet appears never to have seen a pair of feet and there's not a fingerprint or a wall-smudge in sight? Uncomfortable and afraid to move, at a guess!

A certain amount of clutter and mess shows us resolutely that we are alive – and ultimately that we are wonderfully fallible and human! The gift of actually learning to declutter and detox effectively is that you can control the level of clutter you have; so if you eventually find you want a little bit of clutter in your living room, you can go right ahead and add it!

So to find out whether your level of clutter is an issue for you, ask yourself the following questions:-

- Do you know where your important/personal documents are kept, e.g. passport, driving license, bills, house deeds, insurance details, school reports, etc?

- How long would it take you to literally put your hands on any of the above documents?

- Do you, or have you ever missed an important deadline or appointment due to lost or un-actioned post?

- Are you happy to receive guests with only 15 minutes notice?

- Are you able to have a quick 15 minute whiz-round for your home to feel acceptable for guests?

- Do you avoid inviting guests over because of your home environment?

- Is your home organised enough that you can generally find everything that you're looking for without having to go on a full scale search?

- How much time do you spend daily looking for items such as keys, money, shoes, tools, stationery, bills, letters, reminders, gloves, scarves, etc?

- Do you have out of date products in your food cupboards, freezer, bathroom, bedroom, make-up bag?

- Do you find certain areas of your home hard to access because of clutter?

- Do the surfaces of your house act as permanent host to items that don't belong there? Are there corners of the house that are occupied by seemingly homeless items which you've just not had time to re-house?

- Do you feel anxious or upset when you think about getting rid of items in your house?

- Is it difficult to give your house a thorough clean and freshen-up because of the amount of clutter?

Be completely honest with yourself and consider how you're feeling when you answer these questions. If you find yourself balking at the idea of unannounced guests within 15 minutes, or even having guests over at all - or if you're unable to visually place where vital documents might be and feel anxiety and resistance around clearing things out, then it's likely that you need some direction in organising and de-cluttering your home.

Ultimately, what's deemed as an acceptable amount of clutter will change from person to person and is really dependant on how much it impacts you and those around you. Is it tolerable? Or is there constant disharmony and dissension amongst the ranks due to the impossible levels of chaos? If you've been completely honest with yourself you will know the answer that is right for you and your family – and it's quite possible that having picked up this book you're already planning to move a few clutter-mountains!

Justifying clutter

As much as we might want to clear clutter on one hand, it's also pretty easy to talk ourselves into actually keeping clutter on the other. Here are just a few popular justifications for hanging on to 'stuff':-

- It cost me a fortune, I couldn't possibly get rid of it.

- It's a family heirloom. Well... I think it is.

- You never know when I might need it.

- My Aunty Margaret, Freda, Joyce... gave me that.

- I have enough room for it, what's the problem?

- I'm a bit like a squirrel, it runs in my family – what can I do?

- I just can't help myself.

- Those magazines/papers have articles in that I'm interested in. I just haven't had chance to read them yet.

- I was supposed to finish this, (project, book, painting, knitting pattern, home computer course, etc).

- I was going to start a really fantastic project with this.

- I don't have ANY free time to sort THIS lot out, (along with dramatic hand gesture on forehead).

- It might come back in fashion; every decade comes back in cycles you know.

- I might fit into them again.

- It's better to be safe than sorry, (you might just need that 10ml of 3-year-old shampoo).

- I'm going to send these to my sister, brother, aunt...

- I'm saving it for when my daughter / son gets married, leaves home, has kids...

Sound familiar? Now is the time to throw out the justifications, gradually start to loosen any emotional grip on your clutter and consider what it might be doing to you, and the rest of your household.

The effects of too much clutter

As the epicentre of our family's lives our homes are often viewed as an extension of who we are and what we present to the world. If we have mess and disorder in our peripheral vision on a daily basis, it's likely that we will feel messy and disordered. Having a cluttered environment can make us feel like we're out of control; the effects of which can result in loss of sleep, anxiety, frustration, a lack of energy, poor health and even adversely affect our sex lives.

As the single largest factor in impeding any kind of organisational need, chronic cluttering can manifest itself as an all pervasive form of self-sabotage, stealing what little energy we have left and leaving us feeling like we're wading through thick-tar on a daily basis. Thinking in terms of Feng Shui it's fundamental principal states that a cluttered environment is an unhealthy block to positive energy. Whether we believe in such practices or not, most of us can identify with the effects of clutter and feeling physically and emotionally drained through living in chaos and mess. Many psychologists support the notion of mess creating stress, and how a lack of organisation and order in a home can rob it's dwellers of peace of mind, precious time and energy, and additionally cause unnecessary problems resulting from tasks not being completed or important documents being lost. Not to mention the stress and strain all these factors put upon interpersonal relationships.

Stress causes us to be more prone to illness, depression and the development of sleep disorders. Consequently it's important that we free ourselves from unnecessary or self-perpetuated stress by tackling the issue of clutter head-on. So if we can see clutter as a negative spiral, what positives might we reap from a more efficient and clutter-free environment?

The benefits of decluttering

With less to worry about in the middle of the night, you should experience a better quality of sleep in a tidy and ordered environment. This should have a beneficial impact on your energy levels and overall health.

Your house will be free of out of date kitchen and bathroom products, appliances that are either no longer in use or broken, random 'piles' of stuff, (this could cover a multitude of sins!), loose paperwork, general rubbish and unwanted knick-knacks. How liberating!

You will be able to think clearer and feel able to deal with other stressful situations better, rather than having your mind partly on what needs to be 'done' in the house.

Surfaces and furniture will be clutter free and areas will feel more open and organised, leading to a greater sense of order and equilibrium within the home.

Cleaning and tidying the house will be far easier and quicker.

You will have more time to spend with your family, or on personal hobbies and interests. Or maybe choose to have some important 'you-time' to relax, treat and pamper yourself.

Achieving a real sense of pride at having stuck to your decluttering project; giving rise to feeling more energised and positive about other projects and being able to see them through to their conclusion.

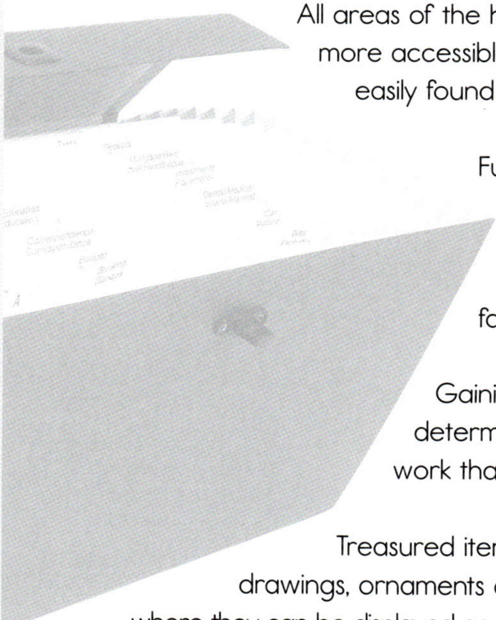

All areas of the house, both in and outside, will be more accessible and household possessions will be easily found and within reach.

Furniture will be used for its original intended purpose, e.g. you'll be able to eat at the kitchen table rather than use it as a storage facility!

Gaining a fresh and continued determination to keep on top of the hard work that you have completed.

Treasured items, such as photos, children's drawings, ornaments and keepsakes will have a place where they can be displayed and will not be hidden or lost under clutter.

Effective filing systems will be developed for household documents and other important information, making them easier to find and safe from being mislaid.

Bills will be paid on time – hence, no accrual of late payment fees due to lost or misplaced documents.

Smaller, easier to misplace, items such as keys, loose change, mobile phones, gloves, scarves etc will have a designated home and be easy to find.

Once you've decluttered and you can see your home with more clarity, the next time you indulge yourself in a bit of home retail therapy, you'll have a much clearer idea of what you want and what you need.

The benefits of having a clearer, clutter-free environment are many, and although organising and clearing clutter doesn't come as a natural gift to all of us, what is a certainty is that we can all deal with it successfully!

What do you want for your home?

Before you begin your declutter, give careful consideration to what it is you want for your home and your family. You might not want 'immaculate', in fact it could be your idea of a nightmare to achieve such a look.
Take a notepad and pen and write down a list of at least 10 words that you would like to describe the feeling and ambience of your home. For example:-

- Cheerful and light
- Warm and welcoming
- Colourful and loud
- Relaxed and calm
- Happy and cheeky
- Bright and sunny
- Busy and lived-in
- Rich and sensuous
- Organised and healthy

Take time to think of your own list and don't feel you have to limit it to 10, as many as you want is okay. And don't worry if your home currently feels and looks nothing like your list – that's the whole point. This is your chance to create the home and surroundings that you REALLY want and not what has just happened TO you.

Ask other household members for their input too, because even if you don't all agree they can certainly have input into their own personal space within the home. You can even allocate different feelings and words to different parts of the house. Enjoy creating your ideal and unique living experience!

Should it stay or should it go?

Possibly one of the hardest aspects of a declutter regime is the decision making process, i.e. what goes and what stays? This can be incredibly hard for those who have a tendency to hoard items 'just in case'. The reality is that most things are replaceable, so if you make the decision to get rid of the blender that's been in a box, unopened, for the last 3 years, and then you decide in 6 months time that it would be a useful addition to your culinary repertoire, then fine... buy another one. This may sound flippant, but it's true that in the majority of cases the 'just in case' never actually happens and if by chance it does, it's easily resolved.

Questions that might be useful in your decision making process are:-

- Why am I keeping this?
- Do I really want, like or need this?
- Does this item deserve a permanent place in my home/life?
- What will I gain by keeping this?
- What will I gain by letting this go?
- Does this fit in with my life and who I am now?
- Am I keeping this for me or for someone else's sake?
- Am I only keeping this because it looks good to other people?
- How many of this particular item do I actually need?

Sit quietly and contemplate any items that you find difficult, be open and honest with yourself and the answers will come to you naturally.

Sometimes it's hard to make a decision because it's painful to think of letting something go from the past. Sentimental items will be an emotive and understandable area for uncertainty, something that was once valuable to us can be incredibly hard to let go of. But we can't possibly keep everything that has the slightest emotional value to it. We need to strike a healthy balance of creating enough space for things past, present and future.

If you're struggling with sentimental items ask yourself how you feel about the item. Do you actually like it? How do you feel about the circumstances from which you came by the item? Do you need a physical reminder, or can you hold those memories in your heart and mind?
This is another way in which clutter has built up quietly and imperceptibly in your home. So, thank the clutter for its earlier use, joy and presence in your life, and then give yourself permission to let those things go, so that you can live your life fully in the here-and-now. It really is okay not to need a constant, tangible reminder of a person, time or event.

Some items can be representative of what or who we think we should be, and not who we really are. Remembering how good you were at art when you were at school, your mum buys an art kit for your birthday 3 years ago – it's beautifully packaged and looks expensive, but it's never been opened. How could you possibly get rid of it? It might hurt your mum's feelings. But this is a picture that someone else holds of you and not necessarily who you are now. And if the item is in your peripheral vision on a continual basis it may also be a reminder of what you're not doing, but feel as though you should be! So ask yourself, "Who is this item for? Does it fit with who I am or am I just keeping it because I think I should?" You might be surprised at how many items fit this category.

Other household items will be comparatively easy; those that are broken, used, past their sell-by date or obviously for the rubbish bin. But for those items that aren't so black-and-white here are a few pointers:-

A quick test is to ask yourself how long it has been since you last used or needed the item.

- Never used – a definite no brainer – charity or bin, you decide!
- Only once within the last 12 months – out it goes, unless its use is purely seasonal and explains the limited use.
- Within the last month – probably worth keeping, but possibly needs relocating and keeping in an appropriate storage space.
- Within the last week – definite keepers! Again, maybe current storage options need to be considered.

Consider whether you or someone else might benefit from the item more, namely a charitable organisation. Sometimes we can get lost in issues of ownership and how much something cost. But does it really matter if we no longer have a regular use or need for it?

It can be a satisfying and liberating experience to disinvest in material value and think on a level of giving freely and from the heart instead. You'll be surprised how much easier this mode of thinking will make your decision making process.

Decision box

If you find yourself with items which you just cannot bear to make a definitive decision on at the time, box the items up with a label bearing the date in 6 or 12 months time. Diarise to open the box up on the due date. Firstly, did you need to retrieve any of the items before the due date? And secondly, did you miss any of the contents of the box? If no, then donate the box to charity. Any missed items will already have been taken out, so you're in a win-win situation.

Ultimately, if you really love an item and it supports who you are, what you want and how you live your life now, then its okay to keep. Some things will just be THAT simple.

Storage

When you begin your declutter regime, don't compound your problems by just stuffing things randomly into storage spaces, (a.k.a. any space you can find). Look at what space is available to you and factor in useful tools like drawer dividers, cupboard organisers, binders, plastic storage boxes and other items that will help you to streamline and maximise what you have. It's certainly worth the investment in time and money. When you think about the storage space in your house, do you have insufficient storage space, i.e. simply not enough – or do you have ineffective storage space, i.e. you have enough but it's just not being utilised properly? Most cupboards and cabinets have room for probably double the amount of 'stuff' than we actually use in practice. There are probably also areas of your home that you haven't even considered that could be used for storage. Modern living has taught us that everything comes already packaged and ready to use, so we have to reassess that way of thinking and be a bit more savvy and creative about how we look at our storage facilities. Consider your existing storage systems, i.e. drawers, shelves, filing cabinets, wardrobes, boxes, etc. How do your current systems work? Look at each room in turn and envisage what you might need in proportion with the furniture and the available space. Your available storage will be the largest factor in determining how much you are going to keep.

If the thought of choosing storage systems conjures up images of cold, impersonal or boring styles and materials, then think again. It's no longer a choice between metal and wood – there are a whole range of different materials, colours, styles and themes that can be utilised for storage purposes.

Get some inspiration from magazines, your friend's homes and let your imagination have free reign. It's all part of the interior design process of your new, streamlined and revitalised home!

When looking at your space here are a few options to consider:-

Shelves

Shelves can be a great space-saver, especially when floor space is limited. Shelves have a versatility which can be used in every room of the house, whether it be an attractive looking glass shelf above your sink area in the bathroom to hold toothbrushes, toothpaste and other daily items, a sturdy set of shelves in your kitchen to hold more significant items, or a corner shelf in your living area to place pictures and other decorative items. Existing shelves can usually be moved up or down a notch to either incorporate another shelf, or to give space to larger, taller items if needed. Instant corner shelving and radiator shelves are very popular and easily assembled. Floor shelving units, such as book shelves are useful for keeping items stored on their shelves and also on their top surface, at waist or above height; such as lighting, pictures or plants.

Wall Space

In addition to shelving ideas, walls can be used for cork notice-boards, hooks for items such as mugs, large kitchen utensils, towels, coats, children's bags and a variety of other uses. Houseware retailers often stock units which can be mounted on walls to store sundry items, especially for bathroom and kitchen areas.

Storage Units

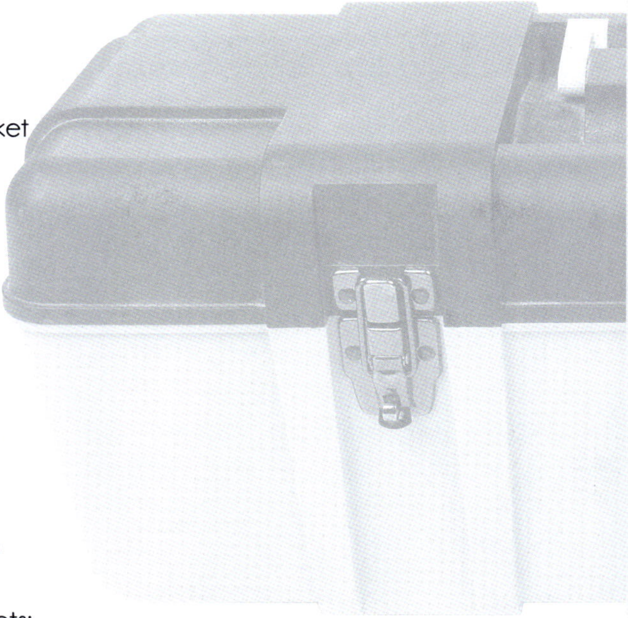

This covers a HUGE market of options for your storage needs. All houseware and hardware stores will stock innumerable styles, materials, sizes and levels of durability. From colourful children's plastic toy boxes and under-bed storage, to storage racks for kitchen cupboards, bathroom cabinets and filing cabinets; the world is your proverbial oyster in choosing what's right for you and your family. Most major supermarkets will provide fantastically cheap alternatives to the more expensive options, although consider your need for robustness and longevity before purchasing. Most of the larger retailers will have catalogues for you to flick through, or alternatively take a trip down and marvel in the wonders of storage solutions!

Miscellaneous

Other useful storage items for smaller and paper based items such as cuttings, magazine articles, letters, household paperwork and certificates may include box files, scrapbooks, ring-binder folders and home-files. Rattan boxes stored underneath a coffee table are a great way to store remote controls and other lounge items, (which if anything like my house frequently get lost).

Leatherette boxes stacked 3-high can look very stylish, containing knick-knacks and also providing space for a lamp, vase or plant on top.

Before you begin – useful organisational and practical tips

Procrastination is often the main sabotaging element and obstacle to decluttering. Waiting until you're in the right mood clearly isn't working for you, so once you've made the decision that a declutter is needed, keep up the momentum and start straight away!

If you're a perfectionist and can't bear the thought of not being able to do it all in one go, so consequently are going to wait until you have several days in a row to do nothing BUT declutter – it's time for you to GET REAL! How do you imagine you got into this cluttered state in the first place? There is no perfect time to start and it can't be all done properly and perfectly in one go. So, break out of your self-imposed perfectionist-chains, there's no time like the present – get moving!

Recruit the rest of your household in your plans. This can be as little or as much as is practicable, but it's vital to get them on board. Firstly, to understand exactly what your aims and wishes are and secondly, to enable them to take responsibility for their own participation, both during and directly following the de-cluttering process. Involve them in creating plans and make clear that they will be responsible for helping to maintain any changes.

Enlist a friend to help – as a non-family member they'll be more impartial and less likely to cause friction! A friendly, supportive and firm disposition will help you work through difficult decisions, keep you on the right track and provide much needed laughter and solace should you need it.

Decluttering your home is going to take a good amount of energy, so know what time of day your energy levels peak. No good getting up at the crack of dawn if you resemble something more like the 'living-dead' at that time! You'll just be grumpy and unproductive. Pick your best time of day to start and go from there.

As well as decluttering this is an ideal time to have a bit of a spring-clean in those long forgotten recesses of your home. Here are a few 'helpers' that you may need: -

- A vacuum cleaner
- Dustpan and brush
- Dusters
- Furniture polish
- Sponge-backed scourers
- Rubber or latex gloves
- Kitchen roll
- Washing up liquid
- White vinegar and/or bleach

A good bit of old-fashioned bribery can work wonders in motivating your work ethic. Promise yourself something you really love to do, eat or drink if you complete a particular goal for the day. Stretch yourself a bit but also make it a realistically achievable task – although nothing TOO easy, that's cheating!

Wear comfortable, easy-to-move-about-in clothes and be prepared to get mucky! Dust will be a major element of any clear-out. If you suffer from any health conditions which could be aggravated by a lot of dust, take any necessary precautions to ensure that you don't become ill. Dust guards which fit over the mouth and nose area can be purchased from DIY and hardware stores. Drink plenty of fluids whilst you are working also.
Provide delicious, yummy food and oodles of love and praise at the end of the day for all your helpers. The promise of a take-out, a favourite DVD and a relaxing evening all together on the couch is an amazingly satisfying reward after a hard day's organising.

Play your favourite music whilst you work – or have a favourite programme on if you're in the eye-line of a TV. You will probably become really engrossed in what you're doing so some great music might be just the ticket.

Pick out a suitable charitable organisation to benefit from items in good condition which can be passed on. For example, local charity shops or local shelters and kitchens. Friends and relations can also be a consideration, but be careful that you don't end up storing things for them until they're ready to receive them!

Pace yourself and tackle one room at a time with your designated team of helpers – trying to do more will most likely set you up for failure, or an astronomical meltdown as you become quickly overwhelmed.

Draw up a rough action plan, (anything too detailed might stop you even wanting to start!), work out a realistic time schedule and stick to it. The rest of your life still has to operate and if you start missing out other things you need to do, you could find them fast becoming an excuse not to continue with your decluttering plans. Be structured – focus your energies, but stop when you have scheduled yourself to stop.

Diarise your de-cluttering time as if you were out at work and let everyone know that you're unavailable at those times. Taking full or half days are probably best to start, so that you can make a significant dent in the workload - but ensure that you schedule yourself in some well-earned breaks! When scheduling your time, factor in that you'll need both organising and clearing away time – perhaps try for 70% organising time and 30% clearing away time. Make the appropriate space for both within your action plan.

When tackling someone else's room, or personal effects, be sure to involve them in the process. It's counter-productive and ultimately hurtful to reorganise someone else's personal possessions without their inclusion. They have the right to make their own decisions and give permission for what happens in their own space. Plus, if you don't invest in making sure that this simple respect is extended, you could find that your hard work is either sabotaged in the making, or very shortly afterwards. It's less stressful and in the interests of all parties to be supportive and agree a plan beforehand.

Types of clutter

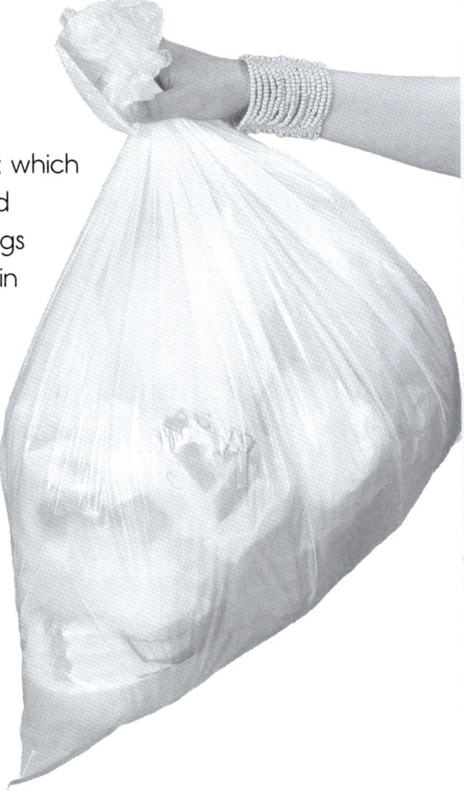

There are two main types of clutter to differentiate between, 'surface clutter'; which relates to bigger more visible items and 'hidden clutter'; which relates to all things small, residing in drawers, under beds, in cabinets, in piles, etc. It's useful to come at these two types of clutter from differing mental and timing perspectives. Trying to tackle the 'hidden clutter' too early can be disheartening as results are slow and not highly visible. Whereas moving larger areas of 'surface clutter' will provide swift aesthetic results, giving you a welcome boost to your efforts. Taking a drawer out and sorting through its contents later on in the process can be incredibly calming and rewarding.

Recycle

Recycle wherever possible – paper, plastic, cardboard, glass, batteries, mobile phones, garden waste and wood.

4 piles rule

Plan where items are going to go and apply a 4-piles rule:

- Rubbish
- Recycling
- Donations
- Items for another room

Any rubbish should go straight into a bin-bag, whilst the 3 other categories should have their own boxes. You will need to have space for each separate box/bag, so create this before you start.

To ensure that the dreaded guilt and second thoughts don't creep in, in relation to your 'throwing out' pile, choose to use opaque rubbish bags!

Once you've decided what things are going, it's important to get them out of the house as soon as possible. Designate someone to take rubbish to the tip or donations to their new home. Don't leave this as an after thought otherwise your newly organised piles could turn into another room's clutter problem!

Other avenues for getting rid of oversized, electrical or large amounts of rubbish are your local council or licensed waste disposal companies. Both will charge for disposal services and can be found in your local business directories or Yellow Pages.

If you have items that are still of a worthwhile value, consider selling them through a local free ad-magazine, local paper or on an internet site such as eBay. Give yourself a deadline for any sale items as this could lead to hanging onto items unnecessarily if not sold in good time. You may have to ultimately accept that one man's rubbish is also another man's rubbish too!

Think carefully when determining where 'kept' items are going to be stored. Be logical and practical in priority over the visual aspects of where things belong. Keep items in places that make sense and that work for you on a functional level. Wherever possible, try to store frequently used items where they are most often used. For example, store toilet paper in the bathroom rather than in the airing cupboard down the hallway. How infuriating to have to get some fresh loo-roll when natures-call is urgently screaming at you! You shouldn't have to be traipsing to another room to get items that you use every day. Aesthetics are an important consideration but this is ultimately an exercise in making your life easier.

Find homes for all items and stick to them. Sounds simple, but this can be a real challenge in practice. Items should always be returned straight to their allotted space once they have been used.

Make an inventory of items which are moved to the attic, cellar or garage. Boxed items should have a list on the outer lid of the box and keep a hard copy in your filing, or on your computer.

Financial data and documents to be stored for a number of years should be boxed with a due date for shredding written on the outer lid. Make a note of the date and set yourself a reminder.

Keep up the momentum and energy – once you've started and feel energised, keep going! Don't get complacent about the fact that you've done one room; it's easy to slip back into old ways.

Pick a starting point in the house and start at the highest level.

Make sure that everyone continues to do their bit. For all household members, use a task rota, this will jog their memories, (i.e. no excuses) and maintain the effectiveness of your decluttering.

Don't expect miracles overnight! Decluttering is not a quick-fix; it's a slow, thorough and methodical process which takes time, energy and thought. Don't try and take short-cuts, if you do you will only suffer for it at a later stage.

Take time to celebrate each achievement and each room separately, you deserve it. Then, when you're done, imagine how elated, proud and dynamic you'll feel. You'll deserve to be wearing pants on the outside of your trousers with a big 'S' on them!

Feeling overwhelmed?

If you begin to feel overwhelmed and start doubting what you're doing, follow these steps to get yourself back on the right track:-

- Firstly STOP and allow yourself to take some timeout. Walk away, get yourself a hot or soft drink and re-group. If you've hit what feels to be a brick-wall, don't panic or lose faith. It's highly unlikely that whatever your issue is it's insurmountable, and taking stock of that fact is important.
If you're feeling tired then give yourself an unscheduled break. This was always going to be hard work, but you're not in a compulsory 'boot-camp', you can be easy on yourself when it's needed.

- Take it steady and give yourself permission to reassess your schedule - you don't have to race against the clock. Of course you still need a schedule, so that you can know where you are and have some idea of timescales. But if what you've previously set yourself is too much for you or unrealistic, then it's within your power to look at it again from a new perspective.

- Get some support. If you've not got someone doing this with you or if you have long periods of time when you are working alone, it can be a bit of a daunting task. Seek out the trusted support of your spouse, a relative or a good friend. This may be to work out a new schedule, band about some new ideas, get some physical assistance or indeed to get some much needed encouragement and validation. Or even just a hug!

- Learn to say 'NO!' Is part of your problem the fact that you have too many other pressures on top of what you're already trying to achieve here? Pulled this way and that and not able to say 'No'? This way of being is more widespread than you think and many of us clutter-bugs suffer from the 'N...N...N...Yes-syndrome'. It's a struggle to go against the grain and risk upsetting or letting someone down, (in our perception anyway). But the saying 'Peace at all costs is no peace at all' is very relevant to this situation and it's time to get a little tougher and think of your own needs. Say 'No', delegate, do it another time... whatever it takes. YOU deserve to have a beautiful, organised and lovely home!!!!

- Reward yourself. We've talked about rewarding yourself with things you like to do, eat or drink – but how about taking some time out just for you as a reward too? Some time to relax and just 'be' for a little while. This can be scheduled in at the end of a particular task, (especially those you're not looking forward to), and allow yourself around 20-30 minutes afterwards to do whatever you please. That may be sitting and staring out a window, or taking a short stroll in the fresh air; it doesn't matter as long as it's YOU-time.

Okay, so now you've trashed your guilt-urges, assembled all your vital tools, rallied your friends and allies and created your vision - no more stalling and putting it off, you're ready to begin. Let the decluttering commence!

In conclusion… Keep it up!

Congratulate yourself on a job excellently done. Can you feel the difference in your home? All that clutter has gone. No more avoiding, no more being embarrassed to have visitors, no more time wasted on searching for things, no more tripping over things and cursing - and no more beating yourself up for not having a clutter-free, organised and healthily functioning house. You've done it! I bet you feel lighter, brighter, in control, less stressed and more invigorated and energised than you have for a long time. Fantastic work!

Now is the time to make sure that you NEVER go back there again, and with these simple-to-do pointers you'll be sure to keep your home as carefree and wonderful as it is now:-

Firstly, go forward with the understanding that keeping your house clutter-free is an on-going process, a way of living and it will eventually become second nature and a way of existing.

Adopt new habits in relation to allowing clutter to reappear in your home. For instance; don't buy something unless you REALLY need it, take shopping lists when out shopping so you don't get sucked in by shrewd marketing techniques, (they do work you know!), don't accept random gifts which have been unwanted items of friends and relatives, unsubscribe magazines and papers that you don't have time to read and don't order samples or freebies for the sake of it.

Keeping up this way of living doesn't have to be difficult or as intense as your initial decluttering process. Perhaps try a one-thing-a-day approach, either throwing or putting away at least one item per day. Or even spending 20 minutes each day on decluttering, rotating each room in turn.

Keep a 'donation' box in a place where all family members can contribute on an on-going basis.

Keep to a 'one-in-one-out' rule with new purchases. For example, if you buy a new CD player to replace your older version, don't keep the old CD player just in case the new one breaks down. Tempting as it is – don't do it!

Remember to tackle mess one room at a time, otherwise you'll end up overwhelmed and feeling defeated. You're not! You're the powerful one – not the clutter.

Having taught your children how to sort and help out, keep it fun for them and don't let it slip.

When questioning whether an item should stay or go, (either a future purchase or existing item that's come into your focus), ask yourself if you really need it. If you hesitate, you don't.

Remember how bad it feels to live in constant disarray? You don't want to go back there! Instead remember exactly how satisfying it feels to have successfully cleared out your clutter. Feel proud of your achievements and revel in feeling calmer, more relaxed and lighter for having got rid of all your chaos.

Lastly, don't imagine for a second that all seemingly organised people are Stepford-Wife-Like and don't have to put time aside and make a special effort to keep themselves organised – because they do! That's exactly why they're so organised!

Good luck!

House Detox - Daily Diary

Day ....

Aims and Objectives for the day

Thoughts and challenges

Task completed

Useful tips picked up today

Things to remember tomorrow/next time

Daily Diary

Day ____________________

Aims and Objectives for the day

Thoughts and challenges

Task completed

Useful tips picked up today

Things to remember tomorrow/next time

Daily Diary

Day

Aims and Objectives for the day

Thoughts and challenges

Task completed

Useful tips picked up today

Things to remember tomorrow/next time

Daily Diary

Day

Aims and Objectives for the day

Thoughts and challenges

Task completed

Useful tips picked up today

Things to remember tomorrow/next time

Daily Diary

Day

Aims and Objectives for the day

Thoughts and challenges

Task completed

Useful tips picked up today

Things to remember tomorrow/next time

Daily Diary

Day

Aims and Objectives for the day

Thoughts and challenges

Task completed

Useful tips picked up today

Things to remember tomorrow/next time

Daily Diary

Day

Aims and Objectives for the day

Thoughts and challenges

Task completed

Useful tips picked up today

Things to remember tomorrow/next time

Daily Diary

Day

Aims and Objectives for the day

Thoughts and challenges

Task completed

Useful tips picked up today

Things to remember tomorrow/next time

Daily Diary

Day

Aims and Objectives for the day

Thoughts and challenges

Task completed

Useful tips picked up today

Things to remember tomorrow/next time

Entrance Hall

Entrance Hall

Entrance Hall

Regardless of whether you have a large entrance hallway or a few paces before you move from the entrance into the main part of the house, your hallway is the gateway to your home. First impressions count and your entrance hallway should be light, airy, tidy and above all, welcoming. For you and your family, it's important to create a clear transition from one room to another with the minimum amount of clutter and distraction.

De-clutter

Your first task is to look at what you have in your hallway and move everything that shouldn't be there to its proper resting place. This could range from a random pair of shoes to an assorted array of coats, hats, gloves, bags, keys, school kits, dog leads, footballs, rollerblades... you get the picture! Be dynamic - if it's not supposed to be there, move it out. And get those responsible for leaving items there to move them; otherwise you'll be fighting a losing battle.

Stairway

Stairways are a magnet for anything that needs to transit from downstairs to upstairs; it's just so easy to pop on a book, a magazine, a pair of shoes, new toilet roll... all to be taken up at some later point. Except that 'later point' might not happen for days, weeks, months even! As well as making your hallway appear unnecessarily cluttered, stairways shouldn't be impeded or blocked for health and safety reasons. Anyone could accidentally trip, lose their footing or slip on items left on the stairway. Teach children that the actual stairway and bottom of the stairs should be kept clear, explaining the reasons for this – and most importantly, lead by example!

Welcome mat

To keep your hallway as clean as possible from the effects of the outside terrain and regular trail of mucky shoes and boots coming in from outside, (especially during the colder, wetter months), have a heavy-duty welcome mat on the outside of your door for an initial foot scrape, and another on the inside for removing residual dirt and grime. Indoor mats come in different designs and colours, which can be matched to your hallway, but don't choose something too light as this will become dull and dirty very quickly.

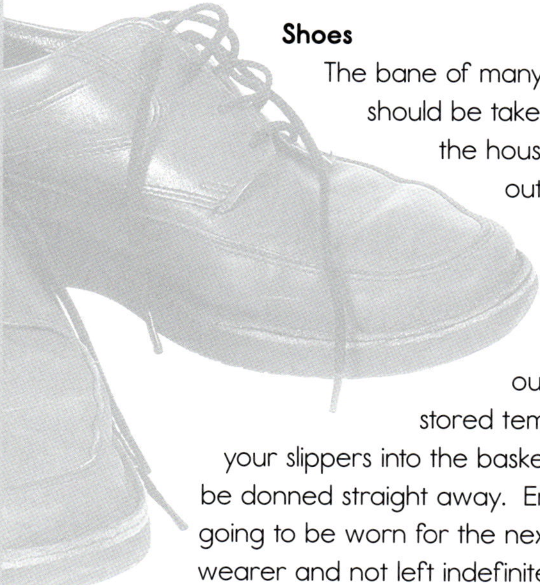

Shoes

The bane of many a homemakers life! Shoes should be taken off before entering the rest of the house, as they will carry dirt from the outside and trail it through to other parts of the house. Buy a basket or a shoe rack to be placed nearest to the door, so that all shoes coming in from the outside can be taken off and stored temporarily. You could also put your slippers into the basket so that indoor footwear can be donned straight away. Ensure that shoes that are not going to be worn for the next few days are put away by the wearer and not left indefinitely in the basket. You don't want an overflow of shoes!

Umbrella stand

To avoid dripping wet umbrellas being traipsed around the house and dumped in a non-specific location to fester, place an umbrella stand in your hallway. As well as saving you from unwanted drips and damp, you'll always know where the umbrellas are when you're on your way out of the house too.

Coat stand / Coat hooks

If your house doesn't have a room for hanging coats, invest in a sturdy coat stand or a row of coat hooks for outdoor clothes. Coats and outdoor items should be matched to the seasons and not long-term fixtures all year round, e.g. winter coats should be in a wardrobe or closet area during the spring and summer.

Children's school bags can be stored on the stand/hooks also, keeping them up off the floor area and providing an obvious and regular 'home' – saving you from stress and whining opportunities!

Think carefully about where you place your stand/hooks, behind the entrance door can make entrance to your hallway tricky, not to mention annoying if you're limited for space.

Bureau / Shelf

If you have the space, place a bureau-style furnishing in your hallway. Something that is aesthetically pleasing as a centre point to your hallway, but also something that is practical and can be used as storage for outdoor items such as hats, scarves, gloves etc. Very handy for finding things the next time you go out. Dog leads could also have a home inside one of the drawers.

If you have a protruding radiator in your hallway consider covering it with a radiator cover, this can be matched to the room and used as a practical shelf if you have no room for a bureau. Be careful of leaving letters and delivered items either on, or inside your bureau, (or shelf,) as they could end up being forgotten or not dealt with properly.

Keys basket or hook

How many of us haven't experienced those frustrating times when we're rushing at 100 miles per hour to get out the door, but can't find those ever-elusive car, house or work keys! Use a box, a basket, a pretty dish or hooks to give your keys a regular home and avoid the drama of having to hunt for them. Place whatever you use near to the door so that keys don't get further into the house.

Outgoing items

For a busy household with lots of incoming and outgoing items, place some nice-looking boxes or bins in your hallway to take care of recycling, charity goods, dry cleaning, items to be returned and any other item which is due to go out of the house. This is particularly useful if your usual process is a well-intentioned charity clear out, which ends up bagged-up in a cupboard somewhere – never to be found again unless you move house or decorate! Be sure to clear out your boxes or bins on a regular basis as this could be subject to cluttering if you don't keep on top of it.

'To Do' board

To eradicate stray pieces of paper and leaving loose notes for either yourself, or others – erect an erasable notice board by the door. Note down reminders for checking as you go out and as you come in. Wipe the board daily only leaving on incomplete tasks. It'll be a useful alternative to the back of your hand or lost notes!

Brighten and lighten up

If your hallway struggles for light then choose light, fresh washable colours for your walls and a strategically placed mirror will add and bounce light, giving the illusion of a bigger space.

If there is a window leading into the hallway, don't obscure the light coming through. Avoid pendant lighting as this will have the effect of bringing the ceiling down and making the space feel smaller, use instead down-lighters with low voltage bulbs.

Pick a neutral coloured flooring to create lightness and more space, something that's tough and robust for all the heavy foot-traffic. Keep window dressings a light colour and add tiebacks for embellishment.

Lounge

Lounge

Lounge

Lounge, living room, family room...

However you refer to it this is the room in the house where everyone retires to, at one time of the day or another, and is where we generally like to congregate, relax, spend quality time together and receive company. If we're overrun by clutter and disorganisation in this area we will not only create a discordant atmosphere for our family but also make our guests feel uncomfortable.

Have a good look around the room, what do you see? Does everything belong in there? Or are there out-of-place items lurking in corners, in piles, in drawers, on tables, under tables....be honest with yourself. Begin moving things out where necessary, into their allotted piles of recycled, rubbish, donations or for another room.

Paper rack

Invest in a paper rack, one that suits the look of your room, and keep all current publications inside it. If the rack becomes full then apply the two aforementioned tips – ultimately, clear them out!

Magazines

If you have piles of magazines/papers which have been kept specifically for articles – tear out the articles in question and file them in a clear plastic wallet folder and dispose of the rest of the magazine/paper. Your plastic wallet folder can be sectioned to areas of your house/life in relation to each article, e.g. kitchen, children's sports, health etc.

If you have piles of magazines/papers that have just not been read, then it's questionable as to whether:

a) you really like the reading material and

b) whether you conceivably have the time to read them!

Whatever the reason for them not being read, it's time to recycle them – bar perhaps 2 or 3 copies of either the latest editions or those that are of most interest to you. If you have a subscription to these un-read items – cancel it!!!

Toys

If there are children's toys in your living room and this is the best place for them to be kept, then organise toys in storage baskets or bins and arrange them in a shelving unit to save space and to maximise neatness.

If you're adamant that toys should not be in the living room at all, but they somehow find their way in, then use a decorative looking basket to collect the toys in at the end of each day. You can choose whether this gets emptied once a day or once a week.

Curtains

Curtains that need refreshing can be taken down and put into the dryer to remove dust. Check the care instructions on your curtains before doing this.

If you have carpets and upholstery that are dirty and could do with a bit of a spring-clean, either hire a professional cleaning appliance or call in a professional cleaning company.

Clutter areas

Identify areas of the room that tend to attract clutter and address them. Either introduce racks or storage options or fill the space with something decorative that will discourage those that leave the clutter. If other members of the household continue to leave clutter in the room, then stick within your boundaries and confront the issue directly.

Encourage children to help tidy the room and take out their own belongings as part of their bedtime routine. If there are lots of toys milling around you can even make it into a game – e.g. who can get the most in the basket in the quickest time.

Think about having guests when you're arranging your living room. Is it conducive to conversation, or is it more attuned to watching TV and being unsociable? Take steps to arrange your room to encourage and promote conversation, you'll have a better quality of interaction as a family as well as being more welcoming for guests.

Think about how much leg room you have between your sofa/chairs and the coffee table, those with longer legs will appreciate your consideration!

Put your CDs back in their covers. It's about respecting your belongings and the things you value. If you don't care if they scratch, get rid of them! CDs cost money. Purpose built CD racks or holders will only ever have one use, but neat, boxy shelves can house books, nick nacks or any other small items. Think versatile when you're shopping for new organising containers. Don't use boxes for CDs; it's high maintenance removing a lid, and then having to return it to the top of the container. Being organised should be simple, not hard work.

Kitchen/Dining Room

Kitchen and Dining Room

Kitchens can be a nightmare to keep clean, tidy and uncluttered. Just by their very nature they're the hub of activity in every household, constantly needing to be utilised to keep ourselves and our families adequately nourished and healthily ticking over. Not being able to operate in a fully functional and uncluttered kitchen is a disheartening experience for anyone and is likely to deter any passion, or enthusiasm in cooking on a regular basis.

Kitchens can also be an opportunity for families to spend quality time together – meal times at the table in a warm and inviting kitchen/dining environment fills an important dynamic in our modern, busy lifestyles.
If we're put off from cooking and dining together both our nutrition and our relationships can suffer. Plus it's hard to get your children to help with the dishes when there's too much chaos around! So, time to get yourself geared up for a new, ultra-productive and super-organised kitchen area.

Before you begin, brace yourself for a courageous and decisive clear out. Prepare to rid yourself of drawers, cupboards and surfaces clogged with coupons, loose knick-knacks, never-opened cookbooks and all manner of electrical products gathering dust. Dare to be dynamic and re-claim this treasured area of your house!

Initial preparation

This is likely to be a tough room to tackle, just by default and the sheer volume of 'stuff' we have in our kitchens. So, take a bit more time to think how you're going to approach each area, and think about these preparation tips.

Clean and tidy

In order to clear as much space as possible, firstly wash and put away any dishes and bring your kitchen to its usually most ordered state of being. Fill a bowl with hot soapy water so that dusty items and shelves can be washed or wiped down.

4 Piles System

Get ready with your 4-piles system - rubbish, recycling, charity donations and items for another room, (as well as items which will be re-integrated back into your kitchen area).

Starting point

Pick a starting point and work from the top downwards. Give each cleared area a good clean before beginning to put things back in place. Give items that are dusty and grubby a wash too. If you're not working alone perhaps you can delegate someone to wash down cleared areas and someone to wash the contents.

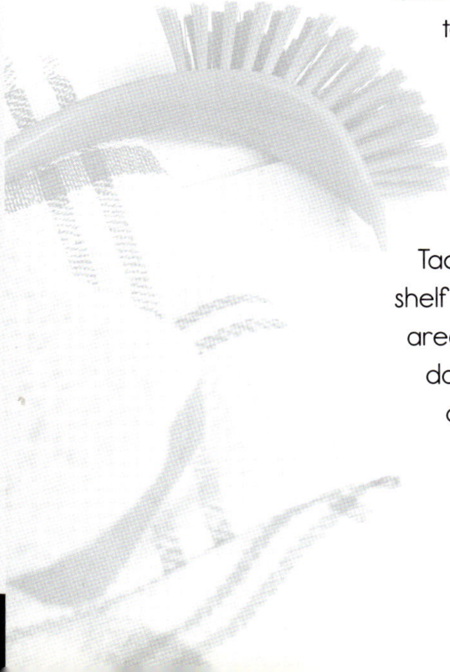

Pace yourself. Tackle one drawer, one cupboard, one shelf at a time. If you start jumping from one area of the kitchen to another you're in danger of becoming overwhelmed. So, one thing at a time and don't allow yourself to be distracted.

Don't rush

Take it steady and you're more likely to make good decisions and not rush into a hasty finish. If you feel yourself getting bored or fed-up then take a break – don't cave into wanting to get it over and done with as quick as possible, the consequences could make your life very difficult and frustrating for much, much longer than persevering with your detoxing routine.

Most of all; be sure to have some fun! Your kitchen doesn't have to be out-of-a-magazine perfect – just start and see where it leads you. You never know, you might actually enjoy yourself!

What's in there?

Because of the abundance of 'stuff' in this room, make sure that anyone enlisted to help you has no attachment to; or investment in keeping the clutter in your kitchen.

Food cupboards

Sort diligently through your food cupboards, getting rid of any out-of-date ingredients, packets and cans. Donate cans and packets that are no longer wanted, as long as they haven't expired.

Organise remaining food-stuffs into categories, e.g. tinned items on one shelf; flour, sugar, flavourings and dried fruits onto another; coffee, tea and herbal drinks on another, and so on. Make sure that labels are turned to the front and can be clearly seen. Keep items used most regularly stored nearest to the front at eye level for easy access.

If you remove ingredients or other foods such as pasta or rice out of their original packaging into storage jars or containers, ensure that you clearly mark on the front what the contents are, when they were opened and the expiry date.

Chipped, broken, stained or cracked?
These items need to go! No negotiation!

Appliances

Remove any appliance or item off your worktops that doesn't get used at least once a week. Store them in a cup-board and take them out only when needed.

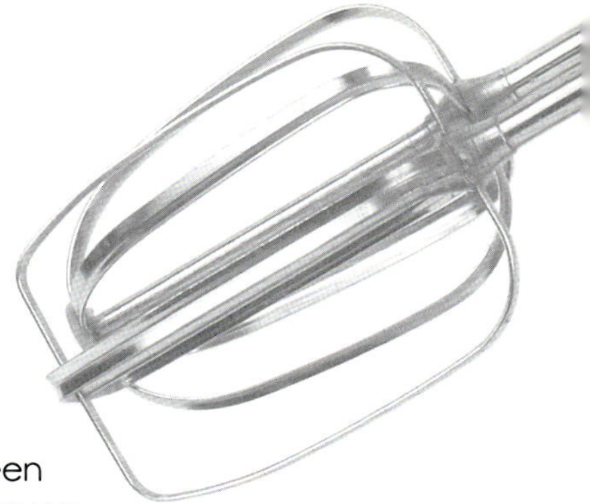

Get out those appliances that haven't been used for a number of years – are you REALLY likely to use them again in the foreseeable future? Remember the rule that most things are ultimately replaceable – so let them go.

Sentimental

Jelly moulds, cookie cutters, snowman shaped cake-tins and other sentimental items from your 16 year old daughters/sons childhood – if it seems like an emotional impossibility to let go of these then try the boxing-up, dating and seeing if you miss them tactic. If that doesn't work then try thinking how much joy you'll be giving another child by donating them to a charity shop of your choice. That kind of pleasure has no price on it.

Charity

Kitchen goods are an essential requirement of families who are in dire need, or of those who are in transition from one home to another in difficult and sometimes dangerous circumstances.

If you find letting go of your kitchen items difficult, take time out to focus upon whether yours is a well-founded need or simple resistance to giving up something that you don't really want, or need.

Checklist

When looking at your kitchen tools, gadgets and electrical items and deciding whether they need to stay or go, consider the checklist below:-

- Do I use this on a regular basis?
- Is it easy to use? If not, do I need to keep it?
- Do I have an excess of these/this?
- How much storage space does this take up and does it deserve it?
- Does this item really make my life easier?
- Could I do just as well without it?
- Is it in good working order?
- Is it clean, in good working order and ready to use?

Many kitchen implements can look really aesthetically tempting and even useful, but in reality they just re-clog up your drawers, surfaces and cupboards. Before buying ANY more additions to your kitchen ask yourself whether you really NEED the item(s). If you're a habitual shopper then practice at becoming more disciplined and discerning in your choices. If you're worried that you'll find the habit difficult to break then take someone with you, or at least keep the receipt and seek a good friend's opinion when you get home. You can always take it back! Remember that YOU are in control of what comes into and lives in your kitchen area.

More than you actually need?

Do you have more of an item than you actually only need? If so, the excess items either need to be donated or put into long-term storage, if they will become useful at a later date. For example, if you have 60 plates and the most you use at any one time is 25, (including guests), then get rid of the ones you no longer like, (we know they're still in there!) and store or donate the others. This tip includes ALL kitchen items!

Refrigerator and freezer

Declutter your refrigerator and freezer! Simple but amazing how often we don't think to do it:-

- Chuck-out any food that is out of date, has been open too long or is no longer identifiable.
- Working from the top shelf down, move items off one shelf to another and give the area a good clean. Don't forget to do the same for the inside of the door and the drawers.
- Different types of consumables should be kept in different areas of the fridge. (look into how these should be stored – meat etc). Your freezer should detail on the outside of its drawers the different types of food that are to be designated to each drawer.

Allot one day a week to checking through foods in the fridge to see whether they are past their expiry date or have been open too long. Keep on top of this to maximise space and keep away nasty niffs from your kitchen area!

Non-kitchen items

Kitchens can often become a dumping ground for anyone that passes through; shoes, coats, bags, toys, briefcases, keys, etc. Put your foot down and stop this habit now! The sooner everyone takes personal responsibility for their own 'bits and pieces' the better. You can't afford for random items being summarily abandoned in the kitchen. Get tough!

Knick-knacks

Decorative items, pictures and ornaments should only be on display on worktops if there is ample room for them. Where possible display your personal decorations on the walls to save space.

RAF system

Documents, letters and other correspondence should be appropriately filed. Create a 3-file RAF system – this stands for Read, Action and File. This will make sure that documents are not lying about, are easily found and are not forgotten at the bottom of a pile.

Kitchen file

To save on lots of pieces of paper clogging up drawers and surfaces, set up a binder with clear plastic wallets inside for take-out menus, recipes, receipts for kitchen purchases, guarantees, useful phone numbers etc.

Children's paintings

If you want to keep children's paintings and drawings that have lived in the kitchen, store them in a plastic storage box remembering to put on their name and age. Choose only 2 which you want to keep on display in the kitchen – and you could even take the time to frame them and put them on the wall.

Organise

Operate a wipe-off calendar and 'to-do' board for all family members to use on a week to week basis. That way you won't double-book and you'll all know what each other are doing.

Bulletin board

Erect a bulletin board on the wall to keep current information, messages or organisational items.

Snack shelf

For those with younger children arrange a shelf which contains approved snack foods, this will stop children, (with your direction), from dipping into sugary or high-calorie snacks in-between meals.

Storage and space saving tips

If you're struggling for space to store pots and pans, consider whether they can be suspended on a wall or ceiling.

Utilise wall space and erect shelving for cookbooks, storage tins and other items.

Carousels fitted into corner cabinets can make the most of hard-to-reach spaces and ensure that you can see what's in there!

Consider buying layered storage racks for inside cupboards – these can be for food, crockery or baking and cooking materials.

Store containers by size, stacking the smaller sizes inside the bigger sizes to maximise storage space.

Square or oblong containers are easier to store and take up less space than their round counterparts.

Screw in a hook near the sink area for hanging watches, bracelets etc.

Larger cooking utensils can be hung on hooks, either on the wall or on the inside of a cupboard door to save drawer space.

Look into the possibilities of mounting your microwave on a wall to save kitchen surface space.

Put up paper-towel dispensers, tea towel hooks and plastic-bag dispensers. Houseware stores and catalogues will provide a multitude of really great space-saving ideas and gadgets for ease and convenience. And it's far easier to take a sheet of paper-towel from a dispenser than having to wrestle with the roll itself with wet or sticky hands!

Cling film, foil etc

Dedicate a drawer to cling-film, foil, bin liners, sandwich bags, freezer bags, etc. Easy to find and makes sense to keep like-with-like!

Old containers

Old plastic food containers, glass jars, plastic bottles, foil tins and anything else that has been stored for use at a later point – keep one of each, (if you must), and condemn the rest to your recycling pile. If they've been there for longer than a month you won't ever use them, so out they go!

Hooks

Hang hooks on the wall for cups and mugs to free up more space in your cabinets or on work surfaces.

Cupboard doors

Create more storage space by using the backs of cupboard doors to fit racks to store loose items such as foil, sandwich bags, saucepan lids, clean tea-towels, etc.

Spice rack

Invest in a good quality spice rack. It's frustrating not being able to see all the different spices in cupboards at any one time – and so many may go to ruin through lack of use. A spice rack will save on space in cupboards and allow you to see all the wonderful flavours you can add to your cooking. For a further space gain, purchase a rack to hang on the wall.

Storage containers

Store pasta, rice, cereals and other dried foods in clear plastic containers, labelled with expiry dates. This will keep them fresher for longer as well as helping with storage issues.

Cluttered kitchen or dining room tables

Kitchen or dining room tables really do seem to be a magnet for everyone's belongings in the house. Letters, diaries, pens, school books, laptops, catalogues, car keys... the list can be endless and ever-changing. Being so cluttered can then deter meals being eaten at the table, either that or it takes a good while to clear the clutter before mealtimes. Either way, it's a bad habit with everyone taking part in keeping it going.

Homework etc

If the table is used for children's homework and/or arts and crafts then provide containers for their 'tools' to go away in when they're finished.

Dumping ground

To try and break out of the more generalised dumping-routine it's worth looking at other areas of your house in terms of mounting some shelves or wall-hooks, so that when family members come into the house they can have their own specific 'dumping' area, which still manages to keep order and can be easily located. This will also help when general cleaning and tidying takes place, as each family member will have their own allocated space to put stray items in, for them to clear away when they are next home.

Table decorations

Another way of deterring your family's dumping rituals is to decorate the table, either with place settings as used at meal times, or with an attractive centrepiece.

Ongoing

Set some time aside perhaps once a month to take stock of your kitchen and see whether you are creeping back into old ways of being. Re-organise what needs to be organised and keep on top of the clutter on a regular basis. It really can be that easy!

Bedroom

Bedroom

Bedrooms are at the heart of our families and our relationships; an essential space for rest, rejuvenation and sleep and a personal, peaceful place to unwind and let go of the stresses of the day. Adult bedrooms are also an integral place for intimacy and relationship; or if you're single a special place to snuggle up in private and read a good book before settling down to a good night's sleep. When we are ill, this is where we need to heal and return to good health. Cluttered and chaotic bedrooms are not conducive to our need for relaxation, healing and restful sleep. If we're sleeping in a room with mess we can never really switch off from what's around us and what needs to be done.

Are the bedrooms in your house a haven for calm and wellbeing? Or are they more akin to unrest and disorder? Are you tired of sleeping with piles of dirty laundry, books and newspapers? Or having to get into bed at the foot of the bed due to lack of floor space? Actually forgotten the colour of the carpet? If so, read on...

4 Piles Rule

Firstly, engage the 4-piles rule of rubbish, recycling, donations and another room – and make space for your boxes. There will also need to be space for items that are going to be re-integrated back into the room.

What's in there?

Take a good look at all the flat surfaces in the room, i.e. anything that will ac as a dumping ground for things that haven't made it to their rightful resting place. Look at bedside tables, chests of drawers, dressing tables and chairs, (a hugely popular clothes storage space!). Starting with one surface at a time, take all the items off and move them away from the area. Put back ONLY what needs and makes practical sense to be there.
The remaining items should fit into one of the 4-piles.

Go through drawer by drawer, cupboard by cupboard and sort through what you don't want and don't use.

Drawers

Miscellaneous drawers; knick-knacks, jewellery, socks, underwear, make-up, products, etc – these are best tackled by taking your time, removing the drawer, and sitting calmly and quietly, sorting through each item. Don't attempt this if time is an issue, you'll only end up feeling stressed. Plus your level of discernment will be somewhat impaired by feeling pressured, so you're likely not to do yourself or the task justice.

Bedside tables

What's living on your bedside tables; do you use, or even need everything on them? If not, clear them away. Don't overload your space; limit it to things you need – an alarm clock, a reading book, reading glasses, tissues and maybe a phone.

Under beds

Under beds; clear everything out from under beds that are not properly stored in storage boxes, bags or baskets. If you need to use this space then invest in sealable storage containers to prevent dust and grime ruining the contents. This doesn't have to be expensive and many houseware, hardware and door-to-door catalogues will offer reasonably priced under-bed storage solutions.

Dressing table

Tidy up your dressing table and only keep out products and cosmetics that you use on a regular basis. All other items should be stored out of sight in the drawers.

Clear surfaces

Having surfaces full of knick-knacks in your bedroom just creates a dusting and cleaning nightmare! As well as making your room look cluttered. Pack away at least 80% of your knick-knacks and keep out only up to 20% of really special items. If you like ALL of you knick-knacks that much then rotate them every few months, keeping to the 80/20 rule. If you forget about some of the items after 6 months, chances are they should be either donated or binned!

No TV

Get rid of the TV!!!! Bedrooms are for relaxation and rest, not watching high-octane action before you go to sleep! It'll make you restless, wake you up and probably give you nightmares, if nothing else! Try reading or spending some quality time with your partner instead.

No desks

If you have a desk in your bedroom, arrange to move it to another room. Bedrooms are not the place for work of any kind or PCs. If you can't find the space to move it straight away then give yourself a deadline and start considering more suitable places for it to be.

Keep plants out of the bedroom; this is not the space to keep them. A vase of flowers is fine as long as you tend to them and change the water when needed. Fake plants and flowers are okay, as long as you are vigilant about dusting them. Grubby fake flowers or plants are not EVER pleasing to the eye!

Clothing

Apparently we only wear 20% of our clothes 80% of the time. So we're wasting perfectly good storage space on clothes that we don't even appear to like! Most of us are guilty of clogging our wardrobes up with impulse buys, must-have sale items, clothes we're waiting to get back into or to clothes that have yet to come back into fashion. So, it's time for a review!

Anything that you haven't worn in the last year should go, unless it's an item worn only for special occasions. Look at the condition, style, colour and wear-ability of your clothes. Try enlisting a good, (very honest), friend in this process. Ask their opinion on each item of clothing. Does it suit you? Is it your colour and style? Has it become dated? Is it too young for you now? Is it looking a little worn or shabby? Be prepared for honesty and for letting go of old-trusty garments. Look at it this way; you'll be making space for lovely new ones!

Sentimental

If you have pieces of clothing that hold special sentimental value to them, but you no longer wear, then store them in a 'special memories box', making sure that the box is properly sealed before you store it away in your loft/attic area. Don't forget to write it on your loft/attic inventory sheet.

Seasonal

Put away seasonal items, either in designated drawers or in storage boxes/bags. This will make it easier to see what clothes you have at the right times of year, as well as raising the profile of clothes that you no longer want or wear.

Wardrobe

To make a super-efficient wardrobe system out of the clothes that you have chosen to keep, start by categorising the same types of clothes together, e.g. fold long-sleeved t-shirts together, short-sleeved t-shirts together and so on. Apply this like-with-like rule to wardrobes, shelves and drawers, so skirts are hung together, smart trousers together, casual trousers together, etc. This will make garments easier to find and separate out smart, casual, evening and work wear.

If you want to take this system another step further you can then group your categories into colours, so put all your cream t-shirts together, whites, blacks, greys, reds and so on. It'll look ordered and organised, make items easier to find and you'll also be able to see where you have gaps in colour, and what colours tend to dominate your wardrobe choices.

Garments should have designated 'homes' for them to take residence in, taking account of how best to keep them in good condition and avoiding ending up with unsightly lumps or bumps, or being stretched out of shape.

Items to be folded up and placed in drawers:-

- Jumpers, T-shirts and other knitwear
- Jeans and other casual trousers
- Underwear – underpants, knickers, bras, tights and stockings
- Socks, folded in half

Items to be hung up in wardrobes:-

- Skirts
- Formal trousers
- Shirts and blouses
- Jackets, blazers and overcoats

A quick, easy and neat way to fold jumpers and t-shirts is to lay the item of clothing facedown and place a square-shaped chopping board in the middle of the back area, with the handle end pointed towards the neckline. Fold in the sides, then the bottom edge and then turn the item over and pul out the chopping board. Voila! A neatly folded garment!

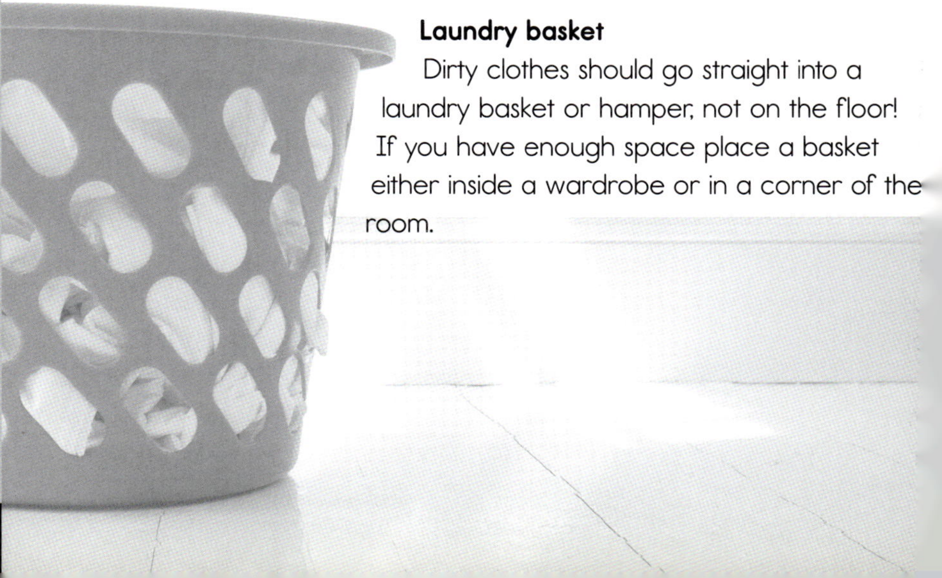

Laundry basket

Dirty clothes should go straight into a laundry basket or hamper, not on the floor! If you have enough space place a basket either inside a wardrobe or in a corner of the room.

Shoes

Shoes; sort through them and be realistic about what state your shoes are in. Try detaching yourself a bit and look at them as though they don't belong to you. Are they scuffed and scruffy? Are the heels worn down? Would they still go with the outfits that you have now? Do they hurt your feet? Can you really see yourself wearing them again? Be honest with yourself and remember that a lovely outfit can be ruined in a second by a scruffy pair of shoes; no matter how fond of them you are. Get rid of what you can and clear space for the shoes that you love. You'll create more storage space and be able to organise and look after your remaining shoes better.

Storage / space saving tips

Shelving above eye level in a wardrobe or closet should be no more than 12 inches deep. Anything deeper will mean that you're unable to see what you have stored.

Use your wall space and erect some shelving to display decorative items, photos or books.

Use deep shelves for folded clothes. For narrow shelves store books, CDs and other smaller items such as photos, or carefully chosen decorative items.

For shelves that are both deep and narrow, use appropriately sized storage baskets to store smaller items. This will allow you to slide the baskets out and search for items without knocking other things over.

Items stored between waist and eye level should be things that are either in season or regularly used. Items which are either out of season or not used on a regular basis can be stored at either a higher or lower level out of direct sight.

Where possible use the tops of wardrobes to keep out of season clothes, linen or seasonal duvets.

When storing bed-sheets place them with their folded side facing outwards, this will make it easier to see what's in the cupboard and to pull out.

Fold bed-linen sets together; duvet, pillow cases, bottom sheet and valance. Use one of the pillow cases to store the set in, this makes it far easier to pull out and saves having to search for each item.

Tops of dressers or chests of drawers are useful for keeping items out that are used on a daily basis, such as perfume, hair styling products, creams and lotions, hand-mirrors etc. But be careful not to allow your surfaces to become cluttered!

Perfume
Always keep perfumes in a cool, dark place as they will spoil and deteriorate in direct light or at high temperatures.

Product overload!
If you have product overload from buying multiples of the same type of product, ending up with part used bottles and pots – group them all together, by type, (e.g. shampoos, conditioners, make-up remover etc) – and take one of each to be used. Store the others on a shelf or in a basket, (preferably out of sight), and use them one by one until they are all gone. When doing your regular shop, check your stocks so that you don't a) buy anymore of the same type and b) so you don't run out.

Organising drawers
If your drawers are big and deep then they can be used to fold up jumpers, but if they're not that size they can be used for smaller items such as underwear, socks, products and cosmetics. Plastic drawer dividers can be obtained from most home-ware retailers and are great for separating the contents of your drawers, making it easier and quicker to find things – especially underwear! If cost is an issue, then utilise old product boxes or shoe boxes, anything that will fit inside your drawers and act as a divider. If you choose to keep cosmetics in a divider then you can order these into categories for ease. For example:-

- Face makeup – foundation, powder, lipstick, eyeshadow, lipstick, eyeliners
- Face care – cleanser, toner, moisturiser, eye creams, face masks
- Tools – cotton wool, cotton buds, tissues, lash curlers
- Hair – brush, comb, clips, hair-bands
- Body care – body creams and lotions, hand lotions, body brush, foot care products
- Nails – nail care, polish, files, clippers, polish remover

This type of system saves all that rooting around trying to find small items when you're in a rush! Take care to return everything to their original resting place once you've finished, keeping your system running smoothly. How wonderful to be able to put all those bits and pieces away in order and out of sight!

Jewellery trees

If you have lots of jewellery but find that you only wear certain pieces it could be because you can't see exactly what you've got. Jewellery 'trees' can be useful for hanging necklaces and bracelets; but a cheaper option is to buy a mug tree, (these generally come in chrome or wood), they do exactly the same job and look just as good!

If using a jewellery tree still leaves your items too cluttered and you want to be able to see smaller items such as earrings, rings and pins, try using a cork pin-board, hung on an easily accessible wall at eye level. If you want to make it blend with the colours in your bedroom then cover it with some fabric.

Use large board pins with bulbous plastic ends to be able to hang your items on and prevent them from falling off the end. Group items together, either in type, colour or style – whatever makes it easier for you to pick what you're wearing.

If you've still not enough room to hang everything, try rotating your jewellery every few months – or even every season if that suits.

Pin-boards

Pin-boards can also be really useful for utilising wall space for other storage needs too, such as; photos, memorabilia, cards, calendars, reminders, business cards, etc. Keep items small or medium sized otherwise your board will look swamped and out of proportion.

Magazine rack

If you're a big magazine fan and you really feel the need to keep them in your bedroom, invest in a wall rack to keep them off the floor and away from clogging up available surfaces. This isn't an invitation to hoard though – once they're read, off to the recycling they go! Any articles you want to keep, cut them out and keep them in one of your household folders, (see Kitchen chapter).

Lamps

For extra space use a wall mounted or clip-style lamp placed near your bed to allow for reading. Keep it looking good.

Hooks

If you've room on a wall near to your mirror, screw in hooks to hang your hairdryer, curlers, straighteners, etc. Saves space and valuable time having to tackle untangling wires every morning!

Clear the floor!

One rule not to be broken – keep a clear floor. If it doesn't rightfully belong there, then do not put it down. It's the easiest way to start up piles of 'stuff' and fall back into old habits. A clear floor means a clear walkway around your room and a feeling of greater space and clarity.

Put away!

Do not fold clothes in the bedroom – they seldom get put away!!!

No clothes on the floor! Or over chairs, banisters or anywhere else where they can be abandoned indefinitely! They either belong in the laundry basket or back in the wardrobe - NO EXCUSES!!!

Gorgeous bed

Make your bed look fabulous, luxurious and something that anyone would want to sink into! Buy good quality linen for maximum comfort and a great look. Using a duvet that is one size bigger than the bed will make it look really inviting and plush. It's the central feature of your bedroom so make it stand out and bask in its glory!

Think in terms of less-is-more in the bedroom. Have as little as possible to clutter and complicate the room, this will make it a less distracting and relaxing environment to be in – a pleasure to sleep in in-fact!

Children's rooms

Before you begin...

First and foremost - don't wade in there in your size 10's and do it for them! The initial approach to addressing children's mess is to introduce them to the concept of ownership and responsibility, i.e. it's their bedroom, their mess and so therefore their responsibility! Children respond well to being given something to be grown-up about, so encouragement and lots of praise are going to be key whilst teaching them to de-clutter and organise.

Reassure your child that you are going to work with them to help them learn what to do and that you will be on hand for any questions or worries whilst they are doing things alone.

When working out a de-clutter plan with children who are of an age where they will understand the concept of things either being donated or thrown away, negotiation is the name of the game. Most children will understand the concept of how their old toys and clothes will be able to help other children, both in their own country and in other poorer countries. As long as they are given a respectful explanation most children will embrace and even enjoy going through belongings to choose what stays and what goes. If there are items which seem to be a real struggle for them to let go of then don't make a big issue out of it – allow them to keep the item and agree to look at it again another time.

Involve your child in this process as much is practicable and allow them to exercise some decision making, this will keep them interested and invested in keeping their bedroom tidy after the de-clutter regime is over.

Work to make their rooms attractive and exciting to them – favourite characters, colours, themes, stickers and materials are all key to keeping their interest alive, whilst also adding to their want to keep their space tidy and uncluttered. Even storage options can be found in bright, modern and child-friendly colours and designs.

Give children plenty of praise and positive affirmations for all their hard work and creative decisions – this will give them a great confidence boost and allow them to feel proud of their achievements.

Decluttering tips

You can easily apply the same general rules to your child's room in terms of surface clutter and storage, but you can also use these handy tips which may benefit you and your children in the process:-

Children's clothes – if you have more than one child sharing a wardrobe use different coloured hangers for each child. If sharing a chest of drawers, divide items by using either separate drawers or by buying drawer 'tidies'.

Donate or hand-down to a friend/family member any clothes that are too small. Although, be sure not to be harbouring bags of clothing for weeks, months on end! If you have a younger child of the same sex, or are planning more children, then use sealable storage and store clothing in the attic/loft – not forgetting your inventory list. Throw away any clothes that are in a state of disrepair.

Toys

Broken toys can be thrown out and any that are in good condition, but no longer played with, can be donated to charity.

Books

Books can either be recycled if they're in an unfit state, or donated if still in good condition.

Storage boxes

Children tend to find boxes easier than drawers and cupboards. Invest in lightweight toy boxes; there are many different styles, shapes and sizes to choose from. Make sure that you take measurements of the available space before you go out and purchase your storage. Storage boxes that can fit under beds obviously carry more benefits for space saving – ones with wheels fitted will also be less cumbersome and easier to wheel in and out.

Storage

When storing toys, try where possible to keep like-with-like, e.g. all dolls in one place, cuddly toys in another, building bricks in another and so on. Put either a picture of what's in the box, (for very young children), or label them on the outside for older children. This makes it easier to find much wanted toys, but please note – if your child fundamentally resists this streamlining, don't make it a big issue and allow them to keep things mixed up. They're children at the end of the day and sometimes they just want some freedom to be a bit disorganised!

Attach rows of pegs to the wall for light toys to hang.

Door hooks

Hooks on the back of the door give children a place to hang their dressing gowns and any other nightwear. Perhaps buy them in a bright colour or involve your child in making them decorative, e.g. a simple piece of tinsel wrapped around a hook.

Bookcases

Encourage your child's love of books by either buying or building a bookcase. Involve them in putting the books on the shelves and teach them how to take care of their books. As well as being a storage solution, it's worthwhile energy in providing something to do other than the fast, in-your-face pace of TV and video games.

Children's paintings

If your child loves painting, drawing and colouring try hanging some string along a wall and using pegs to hang them up. This will give your child a great sense of pride and achievement, whilst keeping reams of paper out of drawers and off the floor.

Laundry basket

If there's room, give them their own laundry basket. This will teach them to either hang their clothes up after use or put them for washing, (a godsend for when they hit their teenage years!). Go for colourful, lightweight mesh laundry bins which can be easily collapsed. For an extra bit of innovation, hang a basketball or netball hoop over the top to make it fun for them to get their clothes in.

Tube-net

Hang a tube-net from the ceiling for your child's soft toys. Children love how this looks and it's a great space saver.

Most of all; make this process fun and keep them interested and motivated in keeping an organised and tidy room.

Bathroom

Bathroom

Bathrooms

Bathrooms provide space for all our grooming and personal hygiene needs, playing host to all sorts of weird and wonderful products, beauty routines, personal quirks and rituals.

Do you ever walk into your bathroom seeking private refuge in somewhere quiet and tranquil – but to your dismay find yourself faced with something that looks and feels more like a scene from a horror movie?

Overwhelmed by clutter and mess; brushes, combs, razors, make-up, hundreds of products, more medicines than your local pharmacy, surfaces covered in unidentified 'gunk' and random items of clothing scattered on the floor?

The likelihood is that the majority of us have been faced with such a scenario; bathrooms really do seem to be notorious for being messy and unkempt. Not surprising given the amount of use they undergo on a daily basis and the amount of 'small' items that live in our bathrooms.

Ideally, bathrooms should be warm and inviting; somewhere that we want to spend time. If you can achieve a tidy, organised and more spacious environment you will open up a welcoming sanctuary for you and your family to unwind and relax after a hard day. Time to detox - cut the chaos and clutter and replace it with a simpler and more user-friendly bathroom area!

4 Pile System

Start out by setting up your 4-piles system; organise your boxes and black-bin bags ready for the coming onslaught!

What's in there?

Evaluate what's lying out on your bathroom counters – and ask "Does it really need to be in there?" Are there items that seem to have worked their way into the bathroom, which have now taken up permanent residence for no apparent or good reason? Items which might fall into this category are magazines/papers, hairspray, clothing, electrical items and any non-shared cosmetic and toiletry products. Sort out what belongs to whom and get them moved by their rightful owner.

Baskets

To help avoid constantly cluttered surfaces and product overload, designate a basket for each household member for non-shared toiletry items. The baskets can either be kept in the owner's bedroom; or alternatively stored within available bathroom cabinet space if the baskets will fit inside. Not only will this save on counter space, but it will reduce the amount of time family members spend looking for misplaced items.

Drawers and shelves

Drawers and shelves should be cleared out and any old products or unused items thrown away. If you've had them there for any longer than 6 months you've managed without them thus far – so be brutal; get rid!

Unwanted presents or unused products

If you have an overflow of products that you either don't want or you are unlikely to use, donate them. There are many charity shops which will be grateful of the donations. Obviously, anything that has been opened or on a shelf for multiple years will be unsuitable and are best treated as rubbish. Likewise, be dynamic about your dust-gathering, space-stealing bath oils, bath salts, shower gels etc. If you choose not to use them, either donate them or give them to a family member; or if they're out of date, bin them.

How many bottles of shampoo?

How many products of the same type do you have in the bathroom? Are there partly used bottles of shampoo, conditioner, body wash, etc? Do you have multiples of everything?

This is a common problem, but easily resolved. Remove all but one of each product type and place the excess in a basket, on a shelf or inside a cabinet, (be sure to keep like-with-like).

As each item is used-up take another out of their allocated storage place and replace it in the bathroom. When you write out your shopping list check what's left, so that you don't duplicate unnecessarily – or run out. Eventually you should only be left with one of everything and plenty of freed-up space.

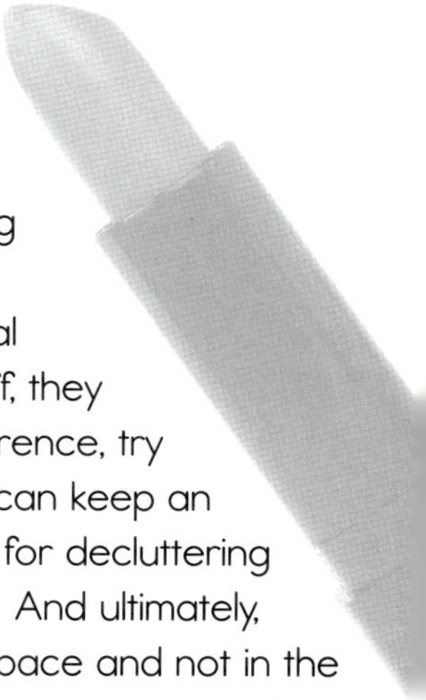

Old make-up

Check through old make-up. Most make-up will last between 18 and 24 months, although mascara and liquid eyeliner will only last around 3 months. Anything past these timescales should be thrown out. It's also important to check the smell of items that have animal products in them, i.e. if they smell like they've gone off, they probably have – so chuck them out. For future reference, try marking the purchase date on products so that you can keep an eye on when they will expire. As well as being good for decluttering purposes, this will also benefit the health of your skin. And ultimately, make-up should be kept in your personal bedroom space and not in the bathroom. Heat and steam do not make for conducive storage conditions.

Medicines

Heat and steam are also not appropriate storage conditions for medicines, so move them out of the bathroom and store them somewhere cool and dry. Wherever you move them too, ensure that they are far away from curious small-hands.

Out of date medicines

Out of date medicines should not be disposed of via domestic waste. They should be returned to your local pharmacy or the pharmacy where your prescription originated from. They will dispose of these items in a regulated and safe way.

Towels, clothes and other personal items

These should be cleared up by their user/owner. Make sure that all household members are responsible for their own stuff – and don't clear up after them, you'll only be making a rod for your own back!

Appliances

Appliances have no place in bathrooms! No excuses!

Knick-knacks

Take out decorative knick-knacks that don't belong in the bathroom. They will add to a cluttered look and will make keeping your bathroom clean more difficult. Dust covered knick-knacks aren't pleasing to the eye and are a pain to clean, especially if time is scarce.

Pictures

Use only one distinctive, large picture in your bathroom instead of numerous smaller ones. Lots of wall hangings will add to a room looking and feeling cluttered.

Children's bath toys

Children's bath toys can create a cluttered look in the bathroom, not to mention the time it takes to clear them out of the bath before you can actually get in!

Look into purchasing either a plastic storage container to store them in, or a hammock-like net with suction pads to stick on the side of the bath. These will not only store the toys but also allow for proper drainage and drying time.

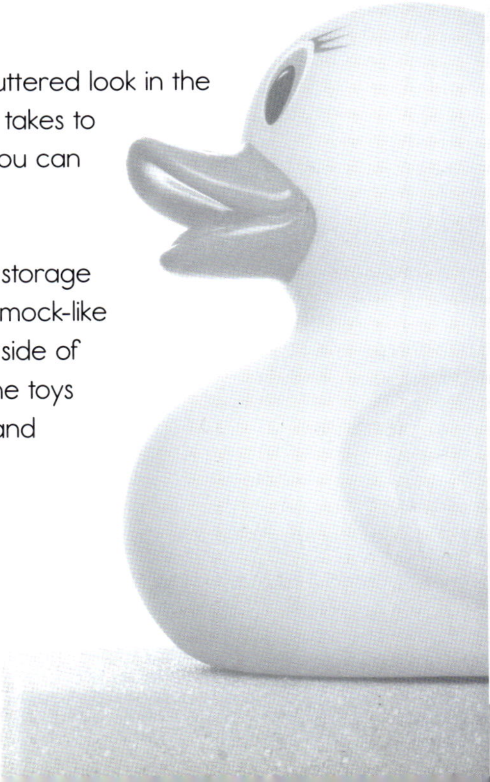

Hooks

Over-door hooks are great space savers and don't take up as much room as towel racks if you're struggling for space to dry towels. A hook for each household member would be useful. You can colour code, label or decorate these for fun and ease if you have children; let them pick their own style/colour as this will encourage them to use their own hooks. Don't forget to ensure that they can reach them though!

Laundry baskets

Laundry baskets should be confined to each householder's bedroom for clothes. Install a shared basket for towels, face cloths, flannels, etc. The basket should be placed allowing for the best utilisation of space, either in a corner or under a sink area or counter.

Toothbrushes and toothpaste

Keep toothbrushes and toothpaste in a holder to keep them tidy and to minimise drips. Clean these at least once a week though, as they are a popular area for flourishing bacteria.

Sink and bath area

Keep the area around the sink and bath as clear as possible. This will make it easier for cleaning and make your bathroom look less cluttered. Shelving and cabinets can come in handy for storing products. Try not to use window sills if possible; again this will make cleaning harder and is aesthetically less pleasing.

Towels

Keep towels and other material accessories in cabinets or on shelves. Utilise wall space wherever possible, or even a narrow floor-storage unit.

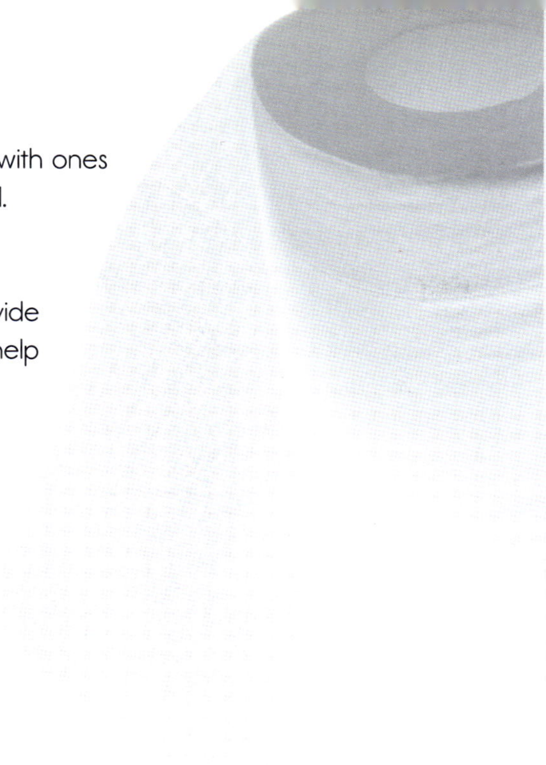

Toilet roll holders

Replace floor toilet roll holders with ones that can be installed on the wall.

Cabinet colour

Light coloured cabinets will provide useful storage space and also help make the room look larger.

Candles

If you like to spend time in the bath surrounded by candles, store your candles in a stylish box which can be taken out and put away again after use.

Mirrors

Mirrors can enhance and expand a smaller bathroom, giving the illusion of more space. Reflected light will add to it feeling less cluttered and 'roomy'.

Light

Make sure that your bathroom has plenty of light, this will open up the space making it inviting and airy – and it will also make it more user-friendly for up-close grooming and beauty routines.

Storage and space saving tips

As a general rule, store items as near as is feasibly possible to the areas within which they are used. Keep like items together and make the most commonly used items easily accessible, e.g. store toothpaste at the front of a shelf near the sink.

Most home and supermarket retailers provide inexpensive and attractive looking storage containers that are suitable for bathroom drawers, cabinets and shelves. Some can even be attached to walls. These can be useful for shared bathroom products, such as shampoo, shower gel, soaps, nail brushes etc.

Baskets are an inexpensive and attractive way to store bathroom items and can be bought in all different styles and sizes. If money is tight, you could even decorate the outside of an old cardboard box with gift wrap or spare wallpaper. Shoe boxes are great for this.

Garage/Shed

Garage

Probably the most neglected and jumbled part of the house for many; the garage is not only a place to keep your car but a great space and opportunity for setting up and organising great storage solutions.

Unfortunately the garage is often misused, cluttered and under-utilised as an effective storage area – so much so that sometimes even the car can't fit in! Here are some great ideas for turning your garage from cluttered chaos to the epitome of streamlined organisation!

Firstly, what do you want to use your garage for? Is it to store your car – or do you fancy the idea of using it as a DIY workspace only, or a gym, or a playroom? Once you've considered your options and come to an informed decision you can begin to declutter your garage space. Whatever you decide to use it for, you can customise the advice in this chapter to fit in with your intentions.

Clear-out

Begin by clearing out all items from the garage using the 4-piles rule of recycling, rubbish, donations and for another room. There will most likely be an abundance of 'stuff' in the garage that needs to be gotten rid of, apply the self-honesty approach and you should be on the right track. For example, don't keep paint from a painting job you did two years ago or more. It's likely to have gone off and if not, it's unlikely to get used again – so get rid! The same applies for old parts for items that you either no longer have, or you can't remember what they belong to – clear them out! You've done without them for this long.

Once you've cleared your space, give the floor a good brush and wash down with soapy water, (watch out for oil leaks on the floor). Rub down shelving with a damp cloth and give any windows a wipe down, inside and out. This area is likely to be a dirt-magnet so a vigorous mini-clean-up will probably be welcome.

Storage / space saving tips

If you have enough room provide a 3 ft walkway, (all the way round), between your car and your storage.

Invest in along-the-wall storage, either free standing racks or mounted racks/shelving. If you want to save money, use old book shelves, dressers and other old household units. Take care to measure the space between your storage options and your open car doors – it's no good having great storage if you can't park your car in the garage, or indeed actually get out of the car!

Old furniture
Old wardrobes and sets of drawers can be really useful to store various DIY materials. It's a good idea to label drawers with the contents for ease.

Hooks/Nails
Large hooks or nails in the wall can be used to hang loose tools and other items, e.g. hammers, garden tools, hose extensions, bags of items, etc. If you have large and deep enough hooks you can even hang up something as big as a bicycle to keep them off the ground and save on space.

Heavy stuff
Store items that are heaviest closest to the floor and lighter items higher up.

Floor
Do not store items on the floor area, this can be a tripping hazard.
Printer paper boxes are sturdy and are designed to stack well. These can be used for all sorts of storage needs. Check with local firms to see whether they have any spare going.

Re-use old kitchen items
Old kitchen items contain excellent storage facilities and tools for projects; spice racks, containers, trays, bowls, jars, baking tins... have a look, you'll be amazed at what you can find - but get permission from the main kitchen-dweller, (if that's not you!).

Glass jars
Coffee jars, jam jars... in fact any reasonably sized glass jar can be great for storing small items such as nails, screws, drawing pins etc.

Organising your space

Provide an area near to the entrance of your garage for changing-over from outside to inside the garage. Make a space to hang coats, take off or put on boots and put down anything that's coming in or out of the garage. This is useful if there's anything that you need to remember to take out of the garage at a later point, items can be put in this focal area as a reminder.

For items that are staying in the garage, group similar items together such as gardening tools, sports equipment, hardware tools, painting materials etc.

Keep garden tools, sprays, fertilisers, mowers, etc together; preferably in an easily accessible area of the garage. Group together seasonal items; such as for winter ice scrapers, de-icers, snow shovels, spare heaters, snowboards etc; or for summer beach balls, windbreakers, inflatable pools, paddles, etc. This will make locating items far easier no matter what the time of year.

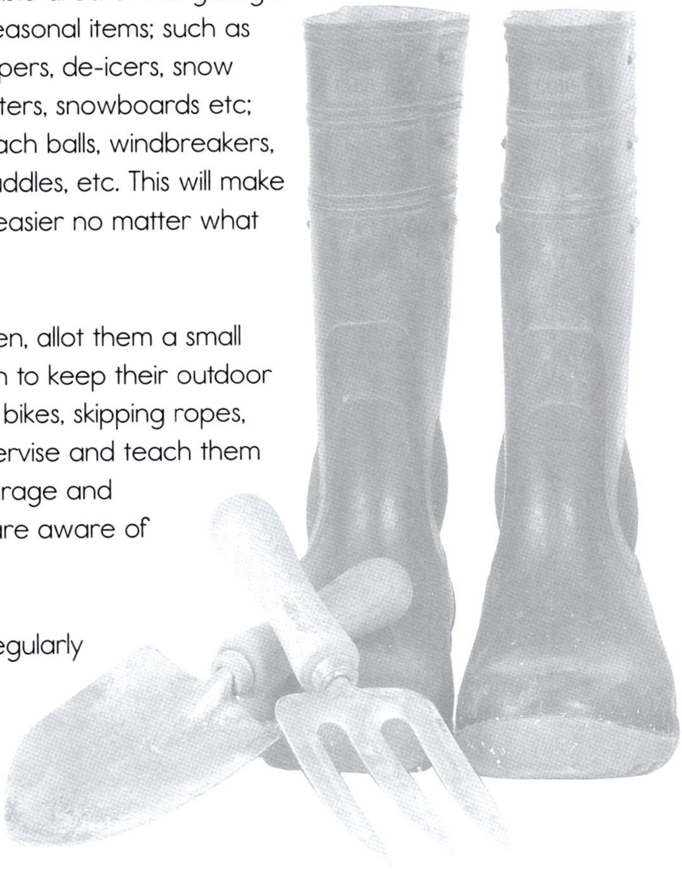

If you have children, allot them a small space of their own to keep their outdoor playthings such as bikes, skipping ropes, footballs etc. Supervise and teach them how to use the garage and ensure that they are aware of any dangers.

Keep your most regularly used items at the most accessible point in the garage, within reach and at eye level.

Make a 'household-overflow' area. Again, ideally near to the entrance door this area can store any overflow storage items that are used regularly in the house, such as pet food, dog leads, toilet rolls, soft drinks, alcoholic drinks, paper towels, etc. This can serve as a really important function if you're struggling for storage space in the house. Recycling goods can also be kept in this area.

If you're a bit of a DIY enthusiast and don't have a shed to create a workspace, then you could make space within your garage to set up a bench and table to undertake projects of interest. If you regularly use this area then this would be a sensible place to store your most frequently used tools.

If you have a project which involves using lots of small parts/pieces, use small plastic food containers to store them in. So that you can identify what's inside them tape some masking tape over the top, or on the side and label what's inside. Masking tape will be easy to remove so that the containers can be re-labelled for another project. Organise your containers into steady stacks or perhaps consider installing a shelving unit, well out of the reach of small and inquisitive fingers.

For tools with long handles, such as rakes, spades, garden forks and strimmers look for storage that will keep them upright and easy to find. This might even take shape in the form of a tall dustbin or you may choose to hang these items from large, deep hooks.

Keep a lock on your garage door, not just to keep out potential intruders but to keep your children safe. Lock away sharp, dangerous tools and dangerous substances such as petrol, anti-freeze, slug-pellets, garden fertilisers and paint thinners.

Index

Index

index

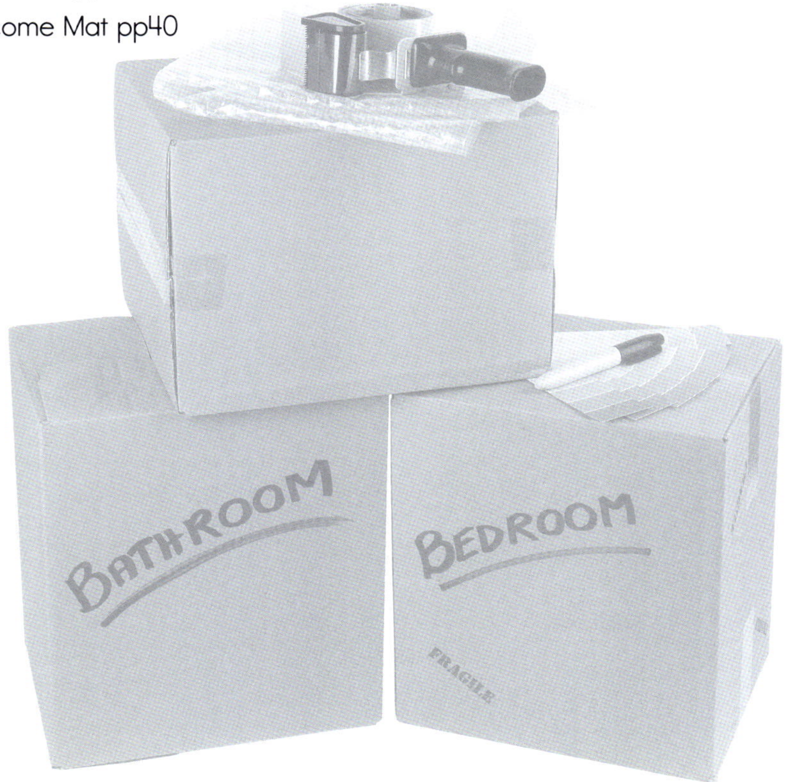
BATHROOM
BEDROOM
FRAGILE

Index

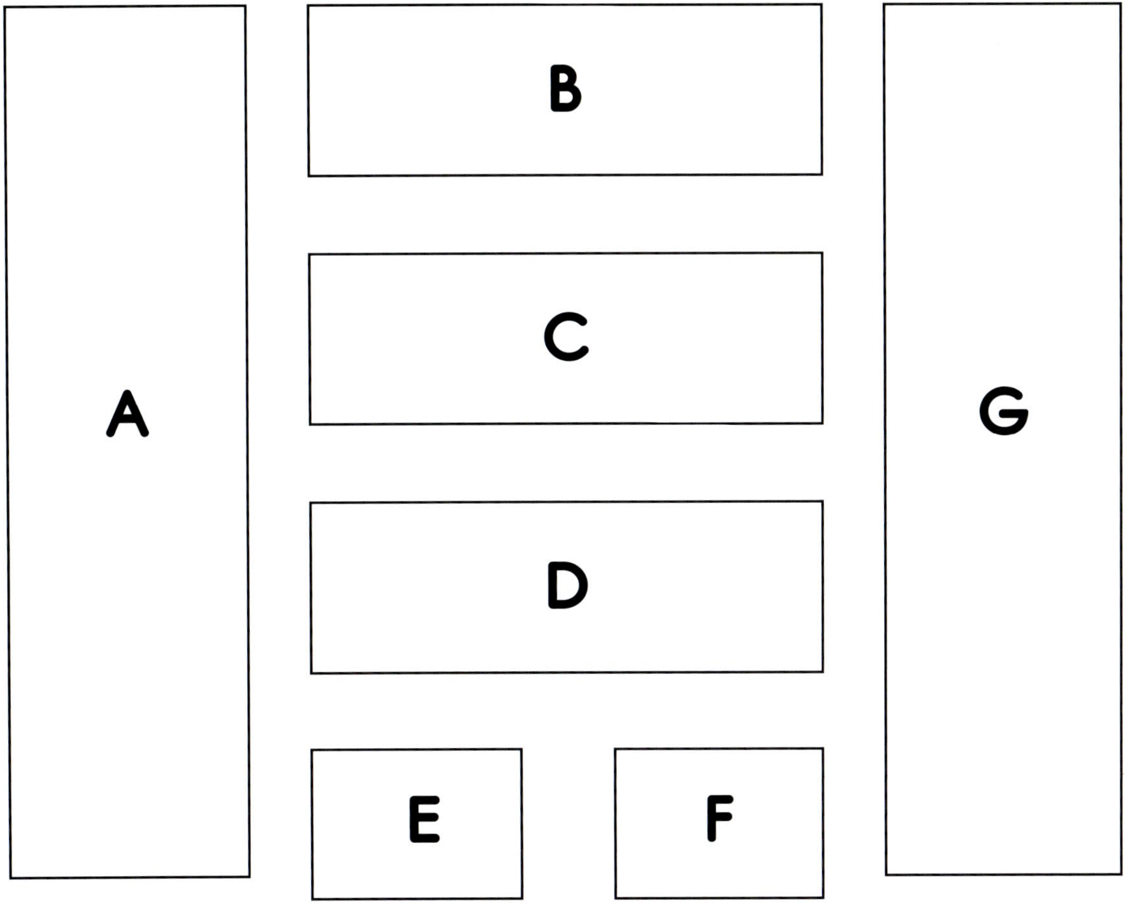

A = Racking - L1 - L3
B = Shelves - L1 - L2
C = Shelves - L1 - L3
D = Shelves - L1 - L2
E = Cabinet - D1 - D3
F = Cabinet - D1 - D3
G = Racking - L1 - L3

L = Level
D = Drawer

Item	Stored-in	Location	Date Moved	Review Date	Reminder Set	Comments
Toys : Ages 1-3	Red Plastic Box	A / L1	28/11/07	2/1/09	Computer	To be donated if not used by 2/1/09
Size 14 Clothes (Mum)	Vacuum Bags	E / D2	1/2/08	N/A	N/A	Keep just in case!
Household Bills 2005 - 2006	Scroll Box	G / L3	1/2/08	2/1/10	Computer	Review for Shredding
↓	↓	↓	↓	↓	↓	↓